MEDICARE MADE SIMPLE

So **YOU** Can Make an Informed
and Confident Decision

RYAN NUTTER

Copyright © 2026 by Ryan Nutter.

All rights reserved. No part of this publication may be reproduced, distributed or transmitted in any form or by any means, including photocopying, recording, or other electronic or mechanical methods, without the prior written permission of the publisher, except in the case of brief quotations embodied in critical reviews and certain other noncommercial uses permitted by copyright law. For permission requests, write to the publisher, addressed "Attention: Permissions Coordinator," at the address below.

Ryan Nutter/Cornerstone Senior Advisors
734 N Maize Road
Wichita, KS 67212
www.advisemedicare.net

Book Layout ©2013 BookDesignTemplates.com

Ordering Information:
Quantity sales. Special discounts are available on quantity purchases by corporations, associations, and others. For details, contact the "Special Sales Department" at the address above.

Medicare Made Simple/Ryan Nutter
ISBN 9798360220077

Contents

Visual Learner? i

Breaking Down Medicare 1

Filling the Gaps of Medicare 11

Part D Prescription Drugs 25

Part C Medicare Advantage 33

Medical Savings Account Plans (MSA) 43

Beefing Up Medicare Advantage 53

Medicare Supplements ≠ Medicare Advantage 57

Enrollment Windows 61

Enrolling in Parts A and B 67

What If I'm Still Working Past Sixty-Five? 69

Health Savings Accounts and Medicare 73

How Our Agency Makes Money 77

Still Have Questions? 79

Visual Learner?

Let's be honest, you get so much Medicare solicitation in the mail, you're not short material to read. Thankfully, we have also put many hours into video production to walk Medicare beneficiaries through their options and help them understand their coverage.

If you feel you'd benefit from watching these types of presentations rather than reading this information, you can go to our website, AdviseMedicare.net. Or, you can go to YouTube, search Cornerstone Senior Advisors, and give us a follow.

CHAPTER 1

Breaking Down Medicare

I often say, "it feels like Medicare has more parts to it than parts in my car." Here's another one: "I didn't realize there were so many letters in the alphabet until I started studying Medicare."

Medicare often feels confusing, overwhelming, and frustrating. I think there are several reasons for this. First, if you are turning sixty-five and are now eligible for Medicare, it is new for you.

You've never been on Medicare before, and unless you've helped parents or loved ones through their Medicare process, it is often very foreign to a new Medicare beneficiary. Add to this all the solicitation, phone calls, and what feels like a thousand Joe Namath advertisements every day, and it all becomes very overwhelming. (Insert mind blown emoji.)

Where do you turn for answers and how do you make sense of it all? I'm hoping this book will do just that.

I enjoy smoking meat. There is something fulfilling about mastering ribs or brisket on a smoker, maybe a little better than the Hungry Heifer Norm Peterson frequented on Cheers. One Sunday morning, I was showing a friend a picture of burnt ends I'd made that weekend. He then asked me to explain to him the process I'd used to make these burnt ends as though he were a third-grader. This made me laugh but stuck with me. I'm not going to call you a third-grader, but like my friend was asking with the burnt ends, I want to simplify Medicare for you.

This book will bring clarity to a topic that often feels overwhelming, so you can make a decision you feel confident in. At Cornerstone Senior Advisors, our goal is, "Simplifying Medicare so YOU can make an informed decision YOU feel confident in." Health insurance is extremely important, and you want to feel good about the decision you are making. So, without further delay, let's break down Medicare!

What is Original Medicare?

Although it feels like Medicare has many parts and letters, if we just look at Original Medicare, there are only two parts: Part A and Part B. We are going to look at what Original Medicare covers and, maybe more importantly, what Original Medicare does not cover. As we begin, please do not get overwhelmed with the out-of-pocket exposure you see with deductibles and copays. There are coverage options to fill the gaps Original Medicare leaves, which we will get to shortly.

Part A

Part A of Medicare is your hospitalization. If you are admitted to a hospital, Part A kicks in. It also covers skilled nursing, home health care, and hospice care.

What It Costs

I never tell anyone Part A of Medicare is free; it sure wasn't. However, the good news is that you have already paid for it. As long as you worked ten years or forty quarters in the United States, you have already paid for Part A of Medicare. All these years you have been working and paying taxes, the portion of your taxes that go toward Medicare paid for Part A, so there is no premium going forward. If you did not work forty total quarters, but you have a spouse who did, then you still qualify for Part A of Medicare, without having to pay a premium, based on your spouse's work history and taxes.

If you do not meet these criteria but have been a legal U.S. resident or had a green card for the past five years, you can purchase Part A. Call our office today to speak with one of our specialists about the latest premium for Part A.

What It Covers

~Hospitalization. Part A of Medicare covers your hospitalizations or inpatient care. Your coverage will last up to ninety consecutive days in the hospital with another sixty lifetime reserve days you can use beyond the ninety days. If you use any of those sixty lifetime reserve days, you don't get them back.

~Skilled Nursing. Skilled nursing basically refers to a place to recover. It is often used when you have had a life-threatening event (i.e., a heart attack or stroke) and your doctor says you are not stable enough to go home, or you have certain surgeries that require more after-care than you can receive in your own home. In skilled nursing, you will have registered nurses taking care of you as well as physical, speech, and occupational therapy until you are ready to go home. Medicare will cover up to 100 days in a skilled nursing facility.

~Hospice Care. Hospice care is an area Medicare has really come through in a big way for beneficiaries. Your hospice care coverage will last for as long as your healthcare provider deems it necessary.

Out-of-Pocket Exposure

- Part A has a $1,736 deductible in 2026. This deductible will cover you for up to sixty consecutive days in the hospital, but there is a catch. <u>This is NOT an annual deductible</u>! So, for example, if you are admitted to the hospital, on day one you may pay $1,736. Let's say you stay in the hospital for three days but end up back in the hospital just a couple of months later. In this situation, you pay your $1,736 deductible again. You could end up paying this deductible several times in the same year if it is a rough year health-wise for you.

- If your hospital stay lasts past sixty days, you will then have a <u>per day</u> copay of $434 for days sixty-one through ninety. If your hospital stay lasts beyond ninety days, your per day copay doubles to $868 for days ninety-one through 150 (these are your lifetime reserve days).

- Medicare covers the first twenty days of your stay in a skilled nursing facility. After twenty days, you will have a per day copay of $217 for days twenty-one through 100.

Medicare Part A – Hospital	Without a supplement, you pay
1-60 days	1,736
61-90	$434 per day
91-150	$868 per day
Additional 365 days	All
Skilled Nursing	None for 1st 20 days
21-100	$217 per day

Part B

Part B of Medicare covers your outpatient needs. This would include your primary care doctor, specialists, outpatient procedures, emergency room visits, and so on. If you are admitted to a hospital, Part A kicks in. Otherwise, any healthcare professional you may see is typically covered under Part B of Medicare.

What It Covers

Oftentimes, Medicare is summarized by saying when you see a healthcare professional, it pays 80 percent, and you pay the remaining 20 percent. This is how Part B works. First, however, you must pay an annual deductible, which in 2026 is $283. Notice this deductible *is* annual, meaning you pay it one time a year, unlike the deductible under Part A of Medicare, which you can pay several times in a year. Once you have paid the first $283, then

Medicare Part B begins to pay 80 percent, and you pay the remaining 20 percent.

What It Costs

This is where you will find your first premium, as Part B of Medicare does cost a monthly premium. In 2026, the monthly premium is $202.90, which is what most people will pay. However, this premium can increase based on your income level from two years prior. This means if you pay a higher premium for Part B of Medicare in 2026, it is based on your income from 2023. If you are concerned that you may have to pay a higher Part B premium, give us a call and one of our specialists will help you find out what premium you should expect to pay.

Those affected by having to pay a higher premium should note that this premium is adjusted on an annual basis. So, if your income begins to come down after going on Medicare because you retired, your Part B premium will also come down.

Also worth noting, if you had a year of higher income based on a situation that is not typical (for instance, you had a sizable inheritance) you can file an appeal to have the premium increase taken off.

Out-of-Pocket Exposure

As mentioned above, under Part B of Medicare, you have an annual deductible of $283. Once this deductible has been met, you will pay 20 percent coinsurance each time you see a healthcare professional. The most concerning aspect of your out-of-pocket exposure with Part B of Medicare is you do not have a max out-of-pocket. This means you will continue to pay 20 percent coinsurance each time you see a healthcare professional with no end in sight. So, let's say you end up with a condition that requires regular treatment for an extended amount of time like cancer (knock on wood). Every time you go in for chemo or radiation, you will pay 20 percent of the bill with no ceiling or cap to what you could end up paying out of pocket.

Medicare Part B – Medical	Without a supplement, you pay
Annual deductible 1x per year	$283
Doctor 80%	20%
Outpatient Services 80%	20%
Surgical Services 80%	20%
Durable Goods 80%	20%
Part B Excess Charges	15%

CHAPTER 2

Filling the Gaps of Medicare

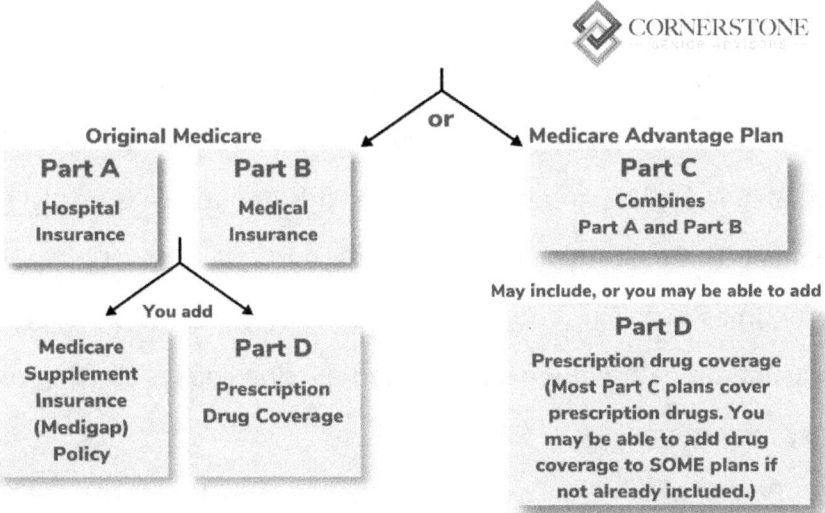

So, what do you do about the out-of-pocket exposure Medicare leaves you with? There are two routes you can take. The first option is to keep Original Medicare and get a Medicare Supplement policy, also called a Medigap policy (filling the gaps of Medicare) with a stand-alone drug plan. The second option is what is called Medicare Advantage (or Part C).

First, let's look at Original Medicare with a Medicare Supplement plan.

Medicare Supplements (Also Called Medigap Policies)

Remember all your out-of-pocket exposure if you just have Original Medicare (Medicare Part A and B)? How about a quick review?

Medicare Part A is your hospitalization; each time you are admitted to a hospital, Part A kicks in. It has a deductible, which in 2026 is $1,736, and the catch with this deductible is it is <u>NOT</u> annual. This means you could potentially pay this deductible several times per year. You also have per-day copays in a hospital starting on day sixty-one and skilled nursing copays starting on day twenty-one.

Part B, which is basically everything outside the hospital, has a deductible as well, but it *is* annual, meaning you only pay it once a year. In 2026, this deductible is $283. Once the deductible has been paid, then you will pay 20 percent each time you see a healthcare professional. The biggest issue is there is no max out-of-pocket, meaning you will pay 20 percent with no end, which can really hurt if you end up with a condition that needs regular treatment for a significant period.

These costs are why you may want to get a Medicare Supplement! The government has designed ten different Medicare Supplement plans, which all vary a little bit in how they help you cover the costs Medicare leaves you with. The chart on the following page shows you the ten different plans, which are all named with letters.

Medigap Benefits Chart	Plan A	Plan B	Plan C	Plan D	Plan F	Plan G	Plan K	Plan L	Plan M	Plan N
Medicare Part A Coinsurance & Hospital Costs (up to an additional 365 days after Medicare benefits are used)	100%	100%	100%	100%	100%	100%	100%	100%	100%	100%
Medicare Part B Coinsurance or Copayment	100%	100%	100%	100%	100%	100%	50%	75%	100%	100%
Blood (First 3 Pints)	100%	100%	100%	100%	100%	100%	50%	75%	100%	100%
Part A Hospice Care Coinsurance or Copayment	100%	100%	100%	100%	100%	100%	50%	75%	100%	100%
Skilled Nursing Facility Coinsurance	X	X	100%	100%	100%	100%	50%	75%	100%	100%
Medicare Part A Deductible	X	100%	100%	100%	100%	100%	50%	75%	50%	100%
Medicare Part B Deductible	X	X	100%	X	100%	X	X	X	X	X
Medicare Part B Excess Charges	X	X	X	X	100%	100%	X	X	X	X
Foreign Travel Emergency (up to plan limits)	X	X	80%	80%	80%	80%	X	X	80%	80%

In this book, I will focus on the three most popular. But before we break down these three plans, I want to make a few quick points about Medicare Supplements.

No Network!

A big benefit of these supplemental plans is there is no network. Any healthcare professional in the United States that accepts Original Medicare will also take your Medicare Supplement, whichever company you chose. This even includes the Virgin Islands and Puerto Rico!

They Do Come With A Premium

You do have to pay a monthly premium for a Medicare Supplement. The amount of premium depends on which company and plan you decide to go with. Also, your premium will go up over time no matter which company and plan you choose. This is one of the many reasons it is important to review your coverage regularly. Because these plans are standardized, (which I will discuss in a moment) it is easy to shop the different available companies in your state offering these supplemental plans and see if you can get the same coverage at a lower premium.

When we sit down with our clients, we show them every company that offers these plans and what premium each of them charges so they can see the differences in premiums and make an informed decision. You know the phrase, "why trade quarters for dimes?" It really does apply here, and we want our clients to keep the quarters!

The Standardization of Medicare Supplement Plans

Something that is very important to understand about Medicare Supplement plans is they are standardized. This means the government designed all ten available Medicare Supplement plans. They tell all these private insurance companies that offer these plans if they'd like to offer a supplement to Medicare they can, but they have to choose from the list of ten Medicare Supplement plans the government designed. As mentioned above, these ten plans are named with letters which are represented in the chart above.

That's right, all these companies that are sending you all of this mail are just packaging the same exact plans in a different way to try to make you think they are offering something unique. And they are not. Currently, the most popular plan available is plan G. A plan G is a plan G is a plan G. It doesn't matter which company you choose for this plan; they all must abide by the government's rules and pay the way this plan was designed to pay and cover how it was designed to cover. However, they can and will all charge different premiums!

This is why it is important to work with an independent advisor who is not tied to any one company and has the ability to show you each option available in your state. We are transparent, showing you every company that offers each of these plans, as well as what premium they charge. Then you are able to decide which company you would like to work with.

Some companies may be a little easier to work with on the service side. Some companies may have a better track record of keeping their rates down than others as well. These are all things we discuss with you.

Dental, Vision, Hearing?

Often, people are used to having dental insurance built into their group health insurance. Unfortunately, this is a hole with Medicare. In most cases, there is no coverage for dental, vision, or hearing. I say "most cases" because if you have an underlying health condition that requires you to see a dentist, ophthalmologist, or another eyecare specialist, it will likely be covered by Medicare and your supplement. For example, diabetes can cause eye diseases, which will make Medicare pull the trigger on paying for your eye doctor appointments. Other instances, like cataracts and glaucoma, will also receive help from Medicare. However, as I said above, in most cases dental, vision, and hearing are not covered. There are many plans available to help aid in these areas, which are offered by many different companies.

Medicare Supplement Plan F

As far as coverage goes, the plan F is very simple to explain. It fills all the gaps! When you combine a plan F with Medicare, you have no network and no out of pocket exposure (see chart on the following page). All you will receive in the mail is a statement of benefits paid.

The plan F was by far the most popular plan for years until the government decided to discontinue it. How nice of them, right?! The plan F is no longer available to new Medicare beneficiaries who become effective on Medicare after January, 2020. Anyone already on a plan F is grandfathered in; you do not lose your coverage. Also, anyone who has a different plan but would like to switch to a plan F is able to if their Original Medicare effective date is prior to 2020. It is just no longer an option for new Medicare beneficiaries whose Part A effective date is 2020 and after.

Medicare Part A – Hospital	Without a supplement, you pay	With a plan F, you pay
1-60 days	$1,736	$0
61-90	$434 per day	$0
91-150	$868 per day	$0
Additional 365 days	All	$0
Skilled Nursing	None for 1st 20 days	N/A
21-100	$217 per day	$0

Medicare Part B – Medical	Without a supplement, you pay	With a plan F, you pay
Annual deductible 1x per year	$283	$0
Doctor 80%	20%	$0
Outpatient Services 80%	20%	$0
Surgical Services 80%	20%	$0
Durable Goods 80%	20%	$0
Part B Excess Charges	15%	$0

The reason the government wanted to get rid of the plan F is because it paid for everything. The Medicare beneficiary had no out-of-pocket exposure. The government's perspective was that beneficiaries with a plan F would go to the doctor for any little thing. If someone has a plan F and they get a hang nail, they could just go to the doctor (maybe I could have used a less gross example there). If someone really enjoyed their doctor, they could go have coffee with them and not pay a dime for it. Not sure who really enjoys their doctor that much, but you get the point. So, the government wanted some out-of-pocket exposure on every supplemental plan to incentivize Medicare beneficiaries to stay home if seeing their physician was not a necessity.

Medicare Supplement Plan G

Plan G is currently the most popular Medicare Supplement plan. It is just like the plan F with one difference: it does not cover your Part B deductible of $283 (remember, this *is* an annual deductible). As far as Part A of Medicare, your hospitalization, plan G picks up where Medicare leaves off and pays 100 percent of the balance. Again, if you end up hospitalized and you have a plan G, all you will receive in the mail is a statement of benefits paid.

To summarize, when you combine a plan G with Medicare, you have no network, any healthcare professional that accepts Medicare will take your plan G, and you have a one-time annual deductible of $283. Once this deductible has been paid the plan G kicks in and now, just like the plan F, all remaining costs are covered.

Medicare Part A – Hospital	Without a supplement, you pay	With a plan G, you pay
1-60 days	1,736	$0
61-90	$434 per day	$0
91-150	$868 per day	$0
Additional 365 days	All	$0
Skilled Nursing	None for 1st 20 days	N/A
21-100	$217 per day	$0

Medicare Part B – Medical	Without a supplement, you pay	With a plan G, you pay
Annual deductible 1x per year	$283	$283
Doctor 80%	20%	$0
Outpatient Services 80%	20%	$0
Surgical Services 80%	20%	$0
Durable Goods 80%	20%	$0
Part B Excess Charges	15%	$0

Often Medicare beneficiaries who were on Medicare prior to January 1, 2020, and eligible for a plan F still choose a plan G because of the premium savings with a plan G. Typically, you can save more in premiums with a plan G than the $283 annual deductible you are required to pay. To compare costs, call our office and ask for one of our specialists. We are more than happy to walk you through the different company and premium options available to you.

Medicare Supplement Plan N

The third and last Medicare Supplement we will look at in this book is a plan N. The plan N is a way to cut premium costs while maintaining benefits that come with supplemental plans like no network and no out-of-pocket exposure in the hospital. That's right, the plan N is just like the G and the F as far as hospitalization goes: It will pick up 100 percent of the costs you are left with after Medicare pays. The difference with the plan N falls outside of the hospital.

With a plan N, you will have to pay your Part B annual deductible of $283, just like with plan G. Once this deductible has been met, you will have copays when you see a primary care doctor or specialist. These copays cannot exceed $20 per visit but are often less. An emergency room visit is a $50 copay. Many preventative services, which include your annual wellness visit and flu shots, are covered in full by Medicare, which means you will not have a copay.

The aspect of a plan N that tends to intimidate people a little bit and keeps the plan from being more popular is that it does not cover the Part B excess charge. Medicare does allow doctors to charge up to 15 percent more than what Medicare assigns; this is referred to as an excess charge. Normally, if a doctor accepts Medicare, they accept the approved amount for the services they provide. If you select a Medicare Supplement plan N and ever go to a healthcare professional that chooses to take advantage of the 15 percent excess charge, you are required to pay it. Supplemental plans F and G are the only plans which pay this excess charge for you if a doctor ever decides to take advantage of this option.

Two quick notes on the excess charge: It only applies to Part B of Medicare, which is everything outside the hospital (it does not apply to your hospital stays). Also, it is currently very uncommon for a doctor to take advantage of this excess charge. Ten years from now, this could be a different story, but to this point, charging an excess charge has been the exception, not the rule, for Medicare Beneficiaries with a plan N. Health insurance is very important, and you need to feel confident in the coverage you have. The unknown of the excess charge tends to make people feel uncomfortable with the plan N, making the F and G the more popular options . . . though a plan N still offers excellent coverage.

I want to mention two major benefits of plan N: First, it is cheaper! It would take a lot of copays with a plan N to make up the difference in premium savings by not choosing the G or F. Second, the premium on plan N has historically not increased as quickly as the G or the F. This is the best selling point for a plan N. No matter what supplement or what company you go with, your rates are likely going to increase. However, historically plan N premiums have just not been as high on an annual basis.

Medicare Part A – Hospital	Without a supplement, you pay	With a plan N, you pay
1-60 days	$1,736	$0
61-90	$434 per day	$0
91-150	$868 per day	$0
Additional 365 days	All	$0
Skilled Nursing	None for 1st 20 days	N/A
21-100	$217 per day	$0

Medicare Part B – Medical	Without a supplement, you pay	With a plan N, you pay
Annual deductible 1x per year	$283	$283
Doctor 80%	20%	Up to $20
Outpatient Services 80%	20%	Up to $20
Surgical Services 80%	20%	$0
Durable Goods 80%	20%	$0
Part B Excess Charges	15%	15%

When to Enroll in a Medicare Supplement

You can enroll in a Medicare Supplement policy up to six months before your Medicare Part B effective date and six months after. You have a significant window to pick a plan and get it in place. To see more information on when to enroll in a Medicare Supplement, skip forward to the "Enrollment Windows" section and look at the Open Enrollment Period.

CHAPTER 3

Part D Prescription Drugs

We have walked through the first two parts of Medicare, Part A and B, which is known as Original Medicare. When you combine a Medicare Supplement with Original Medicare you have dynamite health insurance. However, this does not include coverage for your prescription medications. Medicare is unique in that your health insurance and prescription coverage is separate from one another. This is where a third part of Medicare, Part D, enters the picture.

Prescription Drug Coverage

Part D of Medicare refers to coverage you purchase which help with your prescription costs. Part D may be the most confusing aspect of Medicare with potentially high out of pocket costs depending on the Medications you use but we are going to work hard to make sense of it.

There are a couple of reasons Part D can be so confusing. The first being Part D has three different phases built into the plans which means you could end up paying three different copays for the same medication throughout the year. These phases are your Deductible phase, Initial Coverage Phase, and your Catastrophic Phase. Silver lining side note: there used to be four phases which included the dreaded "coverage gap" or "donut whole." As of January 2026, the coverage gap has been removed from Medicare drug plans, which is a big relief!

But first... What are Tiers?

Before we dive into these three phases of Part D it is important to understand the term "Tiers". Insurance companies offering these drug plans use a book called a "formulary" which is a list of each medication they cover. This formulary also shows what "Tier" a medication falls into. The higher the tier the more out of pocket expense you'll have for the medication. For example, tier 1 consists of inexpensive, generic medications while tier 4 medications are much more expensive and often brand names. This is an important concept to understand as we look at your out-of-pocket exposure for Part D. Now the three phases ...

Deductible Phase

The maximum deductible for 2026 is $615. Some Part D plans can have a lower or even a $0 deductible but come with a higher premium. Most plans that have a deductible do not require an individual to meet this deductible before they help with their medication costs if their medications fall in tiers 1 or 2. This means if each medication you use falls into Tier 1 or 2, (typically these are cheaper generic medications), you will pay the same copay in your deductible phase as you would outside of your deductible phase. In short, the deductible would not affect you or your out-of-pocket costs (your copays that you pay at the pharmacy).

If you do use a medication which is considered tier 3 or higher, then the deductible will affect you. You will have to pay the full cost of any tier 3 or higher medication until you have paid the deductible in full. Once you have paid off your deductible, the insurance company will kick in and begin to help with these higher tiered medications which means your copay (the price you pay at the pharmacy) will significantly decrease.

Sometimes, individuals who do use more expensive medications rely on a Part D drug plan with no deductible. These plans often come at a much higher monthly premium but can be a good option for someone because the higher premium is offset by skipping the deductible phase.

Initial Coverage

Once you have paid your deductible, you reach the initial coverage phase. In this phase, the insurance company pays significantly more for your medications and you, in turn, pay less. Your tier 3 and higher medications are now reduced to a copay rather than paying the full cost at the pharmacy. To reiterate, tier 1 and 2 medications are often already little to no copay and this will not change. Tier 3 and higher at this point receive significant help so your costs are reduced.

Many Medicare beneficiaries stay in these first two phases all year. For those who are on medications which are tier 3 or higher and tend to be more expensive we have a third and final phase.

Catastrophic Coverage

The Catastrophic Phase! Though this phase sounds pretty, well, catastrophic, it actually helps substantially limit a Medicare beneficiaries' out of pocket costs. As of January 2026 this third and final phase acts as a maximum out of pocket. This is insurance talk, which basically means you will have no more out of pocket costs for your medications found on your plan's formulary for the rest of the calendar year. You will pay no more than $2,100 a year for medications, which includes what you pay for your deductible in the first phase and copays in the second phase. In the Catastrophic Phase, the insurance plan, Medicare and the Drug manufacturers pick up the full cost of covered medications for the rest of the calendar year. It is important to note, this max out of pocket only applies to medications on your plan formulary. You are still responsible for the cost of all medications not on your plans formulary.

You will stay in the Catastrophic Phase until we reach January 1 of the following year when we start over again with the Deductible Phase. What a vicious cycle, right?

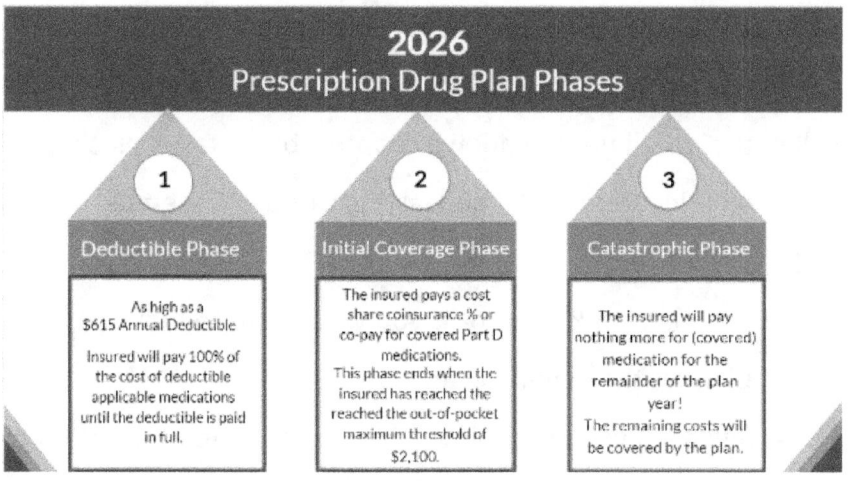

Remember when I wrote that this was confusing? Goodness. how do you make this up?! If I haven't lost you at this point and you are still reading this chapter on Part D, I commend you. Also, I have a little more to explain, so take another drink of coffee and stay with me!

Part D is a Moving Target

I noted before there are two aspects of Part D that make it confusing. The three phases of Part D is the first. The second is that Part D drug plans are moving targets. What I mean by this is these Part D plans change every year. Every Part D plan offered in your state can change what premium they charge, what medications they cover, how well they cover medications and even what pharmacies they work with every year.

We have not discussed the Annual Election Period yet (we will in the enrollment windows chapter) but it takes place each year beginning October 15 and lasting through December 7. This is the time of year you can review your Part D drug plan and decide if you want to keep it or if you would like to move to a different plan for the coming year.

At this point you probably realize it is extremely important to review your Drug plan each year during the Annual Election Period. Part D is a part of Medicare you could easily find yourself paying more out of pocket than you should if you do not review your coverage annually.

We Can Help!

The easiest way to find what Part D plan is the best for you on an annual basis is to call our office and speak to one of our Medicare Specialists. We will plug each medication you use into our computer as well as how many milligrams you take each day and what pharmacy you use. We will run this information through every available drug plan in your area to determine which one will be the lowest out of pocket cost for you each given year.

We will break down what tier each of your medications fall into. We determine if you could hit the third and final phase (catastrophic coverage) and if you do, what month you hit the maximum out-of-pocket cost. Don't try to go at this alone. Allow us to be a free resource for you as you navigate these Part D waters on an annual basis. This is what we do everyday and we are here to help!

CHAPTER 4

Part C Medicare Advantage

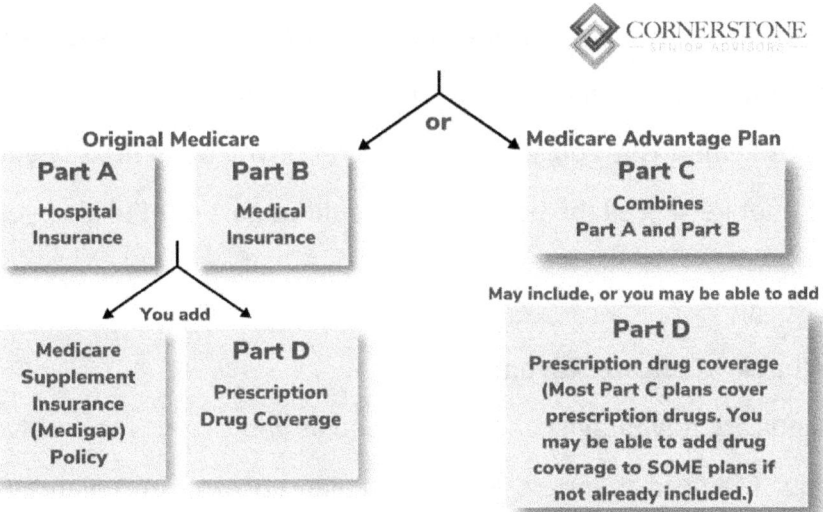

We just covered the first route you can take in filling the gaps of Medicare, a Medicare Supplement with a Part D drug plan. Now we will cover the other option which is Part C also known as Medicare Advantage.

If you have seen Joe Namath, JJ Walker, George Foreman, and probably several other celebrities on TV talking about Medicare, they are talking about Medicare Advantage. Not sure why they haven't asked me yet; I guess Joe did throw a few more touchdowns than I did. It is amazing how often these commercials air, especially during the Annual Election Period (October 15 through December 7). If you try to watch an episode of *Bonanza*, you spend half the time listening to Medicare!

Please do not confuse Medicare Supplements with Medicare Advantage. You cannot have both, and Medicare Advantage is not the same thing as a Medicare Supplement!

So, what is Medicare Advantage, and why does Joe say you are not getting all the benefits you could be getting? I'm glad you asked!

What is Medicare Advantage

Medicare Advantage can be described as another way to receive your Medicare benefits. When you sign up with an Advantage plan, the government is handing responsibility for your healthcare off to a private insurance company. Let's say you sign up for ABC Insurance company's Medicare Advantage plan. ABC Insurance company is now entirely responsible for administering your healthcare. By law, the companies offering these Advantage plans must be at least as good as Original Medicare.

So anything Original Medicare covers will be covered by the company offering the Medicare Advantage plan to the same degree. The "advantage" is they often offer additional benefits.

The Advantages to Medicare Advantage Cost

One of the biggest advantages of Medicare Advantage is its lower premium cost. MA plans can often be as little as $0 premium plans! How can they do this? Trust me, they still make their money. When you sign up for an MA plan, you still pay your part B premium (remember this is $202.90 a month for 2026). But since the MA company is managing your healthcare, they get the $202.90 a month. There are plans out there that will offer what is called "Part B giveback" which means they even reduce the amount of Part B premium you pay. Be careful with these as you typically are giving up benefits when they reduce your Part B premium.

The amount of subsidy the insurance company offering the Medicare Advantage plan receives is based on the population of the area where the plan is being offered and the company's star rating. This is one of the reasons Advantage plans are not as beneficial for Medicare beneficiaries in rural areas. The companies offering these plans do not get as much subsidy which means the benefits just aren't as rich in smaller populated areas. Finding hospitals that accept the Medicare Advantage plan has also been an issue.

Also, the government is going to subsidize the insurance company each month you have their plan. The government is basically rolling the dice, believing in the long run they will save money because they don't have to pay for any of your claims.

Extra Benefits

Unlike Original Medicare, many of these plans also include your Part D drug coverage at no cost. If an MA plan offers drug coverage, it is called an MAPD plan (Medicare Advantage Prescription Drug). Note, the Part D plan built into the MAPD plan will work the same way as your Part D plan we already discussed, meaning they have all the same phases. They may or may not have a deductible, but they will all have the initial coverage and catastrophic phases.

MA plans also go beyond offering smaller premiums and having drug coverage built into the plans. They usually include dental, vision, and hearing. Other examples of what they offer would be fitness plans (with free access to gyms), a certain dollar allowance for over-the-counter items, and meals after inpatient hospital stays, among other things.

Not every MA plan offers each of these benefits, and plans that do offer these benefits can change those offerings each year. Be sure to stay on top of the benefits being offered with plans you are looking at on an annual basis to get the coverage you are looking for.

The Disadvantages to Medicare Advantage

We've seen some of the advantages to Medicare Advantage plans, but they do have their disadvantages as well, which are important to note.

They are Network Plans.

Unlike Original Medicare with a Supplement, MA plans are network plans. This means not every healthcare professional in your area will take every MA plan. It is important to do your homework before signing up with an MA plan to make sure any healthcare provider you may see each year accepts the plan you are considering enrolling in. This is the downside of all those Joe Namath commercials I mentioned earlier. Medicare beneficiaries can get sucked into these advertisements wanting cheaper plans, free dental, gym memberships, and so on, but realize after enrolling in the plan that not all their doctors are in-network.

Because MA plans have networks, they vary depending on what area you reside in. Typically, the plans are designated by county. If you move out of a county, you will have a Special Enrollment Period to sign up with a plan that is offered in the county you just moved to.

They Have More Out-of-Pocket Exposure.

MA plans are going to have more out-of-pocket exposure than Original Medicare with a Supplement. You will have more copays, potential deductibles, and coinsurance for healthcare services. However, they do have a maximum out-of-pocket. For example, let's say you have an MA plan with a max out-of-pocket of $5,000. If you were to end up with cancer, often with an MA plan you are going to pay 20 percent coinsurance every time you go in for treatment like chemo and radiation. Once you have paid $5,000 out-of-pocket, you won't pay any further out-of-pocket costs the rest of that calendar year for any treatment. When January 1 hits, everything resets and you will once again have copays until you hit that year's max out of pocket.

They are Moving Targets.

Remember how I described your drug plans (Part D) as moving targets because they change every year? MA plans are the same way. Each year, the insurance companies that offer these MA plans can change in many ways. For instance, healthcare providers can choose to leave a plan's network, or your out-of-pocket exposure can increase because a plan raises their copays, deductibles, and max out-of-pocket limits. They can also change the extra benefits they offer like whether or not a plan offers dental coverage or if they offer over-the-counter benefits and so on. They can even add or take away a premium amount for the plans! You do not want to be caught off guard if your plan reduces benefits and you did not realize it. It is extremely important to review your MA plan each year during the Annual Election Period which is October 15-December 7. When you speak with a specialist from our office, we will help ensure you get the coverage that best fits your needs on an annual basis!

Three Things to Look at Before Ever Enrolling in a Medicare Advantage Plan

Anytime I discuss MA coverage with a client, I tell them there are three things we need to investigate before we pull the trigger on an MA plan.

1. **Network.** As I mentioned earlier, it is very important to make sure any healthcare provider you MAY see in a year accepts the plan you want. We go beyond your routine providers and make sure we check all hospitals and specialists you may use to ensure they take the MA plan we are looking at.

2. **Drug coverage.** When you go with Original Medicare and a Supplement, you can choose from many different drug plans to determine which plan best covers your medications. When you go with an MAPD plan (an Advantage plan that includes drug coverage), the drug coverage that comes with that plan is what you get. Therefore, before you ever sign up with that MAPD plan, you want to ensure it covers your medications well.

3. **Reputation.** What do I mean by reputation? This goes back to the fact that it is the private insurance company now managing your healthcare. This means if a doctor wants to prescribe a procedure or test for you, they must get the green light from the company you have your MA plan through before they can proceed. Some companies can be easier to work with than others. Some companies make

doctors jump through more hoops than others. This is where our professional in our office will help you navigate your options as we have a lot of experience with many of the different MA providers. We can share our experiences with you and even tell you what companies we would be willing to sign our own moms up with. The last thing you want when going through a health issue is having to deal with an insurance company causing a stink with getting you treatment.

Types of Networks

MA plans are network plans, meaning not every healthcare professional in your area will take every plan. There are many different types of networks; I am going to discuss two of the more popular network plans with you.

HMO

I typically suggest people not go with an HMO unless they really know and trust their primary care doctor because they are viewed as your gatekeeper in this type of plan. This means they must give you a referral to see any specialists. The network size of healthcare workers that accept HMO plans also tends to be smaller than other types of networks. Though HMOs are a little more limiting than other types of network plans, they can offer extra benefits. You could get better dental and vision coverage with an HMO plan. They could offer added benefits on over-the-counter items and a lesser premium (or even a little Part B give back as mentioned earlier). HMO plans will not pay if you go to a doctor outside of your network unless it is an emergency.

PPO

PPO plans are more flexible than HMO plans, and they tend to have bigger networks. If you want to see a specialist, you can go without a referral from your primary care doctor. They will also offer some out-of-network coverage where HMOs do not. A PPO plan typically will not pay as well out-of-network as they do in-network, but they do still help out. You may have two different max out-of-pockets with a PPO plan. For example, if you stay in-network, your max out-of-pocket may be something like $5,000, whereas if you go out-of-network, your max out-of-pocket could increase to $10,000. So, if you were to end up with cancer and wanted to go to an out-of-network clinic like MD Anderson, with a PPO you can go, you are just going to pay a higher cost of coinsurance until you hit your max out-of-pocket.

CHAPTER 5

Medical Savings Account Plans (MSA)

Medical Savings Account plans have not been available as long as the other types of Medicare Advantage plans, but I wanted to devote a chapter to this option because I believe it offers real value for some Medicare beneficiaries. It will gain momentum the longer this plan is on the market. An MSA is a type of Medicare Advantage plan, but I really look at it as a hybrid between your typical Medicare Advantage plans and your Medicare Supplement plans. It pulls benefits from both sides.

Like other Advantage plans, the company you use when signing up for the MSA plan is now solely responsible for your healthcare. This means you still pay the Part B premium, which in 2026 is $202.90 a month, but this premium goes to the company you select when signing up for the MSA plan. These plans typically do not charge any premium beyond the $202.90 Part B premium.

Like Medicare Supplement plans, there is not a network with MSA plans. You can use this plan anywhere in the United States that accepts Medicare. The catch is a doctor that accepts Medicare can choose to opt out of the MSA plan, meaning they decide not to take the plan. However, this has not been a big issue for our office to this point which I believe is due to the fact MSAs pay the same as Medicare.

Also, like Medicare Supplement plans, these MSA plans do not come with prescription drug coverage. This means you will have to get a stand-alone Prescription Drug plan (Part D) to cover your medications.

How It Works

I often describe an MSA as Medicare's version of an HSA (maybe this helps if you are familiar with HSAs). When you sign up for an MSA, you will receive two cards, your health insurance card and a debit card. The company administering your MSA plan will take some of the subsidy they receive from the government and open a bank account in your name. It will be tied to your debit card. That's right, you receive the money directly and can decide how the funds are used for yourself. This is the only Medicare plan which gives you, the beneficiary, money. You can then use the funds on that debit card to pay for your healthcare services. Keep in mind, the funds will only remain non-taxable if used on qualified health expenses. The plan also has an annual deductible. Once you have paid off this deductible, the company administering the plan will then pay 100 percent of your healthcare expenses which Original Medicare covers. The good news is any funds you use on the debit card count towards the deductible! Let me give you an example:

Let's say your MSA puts $2,000 in your bank account on January 1 and your plan has a $5,000 deductible. When you use your $2,000 deposit for anything healthcare related, which Original Medicare typically covers, it counts towards your deductible. This means your potential out-of-pocket is $3,000 in a year, the difference between the $5,000 deductible and the $2,000 in your bank account. However, let's say you go the entire year and only use $1,000 from your account which leaves you with $1,000 left in your account. The money you did not use rolls over to the next year while you also get another $2,000 on the card January 1. You now have $3,000 in your account with a $5,000 deductible. Your account value can grow each year and potentially even eclipse your deductible amount.

Benefits of MSA plans

There are many benefits with these MSA plans, let's name some of them:

1. You have more control of the Medicare funds you've paid into. Since the company administering the MSA plan puts some of the subsidies they receive from the government in a medical savings account for you, you can decide how and when you would like to use those funds. I have clients with MSA plans that have gone several years without using any of the money in their account. They just pay for healthcare services out of pocket to save these funds. Regardless of how you decide to use these funds, you're the one making the decision.

2. You can even use these MSA funds for healthcare-related services not covered by Medicare. For example, you could use these funds for a new pair of glasses, a crown at the dentist, or even for medications! The catch here is when you use this money to pay for things Medicare does not typically cover it will not count towards your deductible. This means your potential out-of-pocket increases. I should also note, if you use any of the funds from your account on anything

which is not medically related, you will be penalized on your taxes.

3. You pick your own drug plan. Some may look at these plans not coming with drug coverage included as a negative, but it can be a positive. With MAPD plans, you must use the drug plan built into these advantage plans. With an MSA, you can pick from all the available stand-alone drug plans in your area and decide which drug plan best fits your needs. You can also change your drug plan each year in the Annual Election Period to ensure you always have the right plan for your needs. As noted above, you can even use the money placed in your bank account to pay the premium and copays for your medications.

4. If you were to pass away and there is still money left in your account, this money goes to a beneficiary.

5. You can even invest these funds through the bank your account is set up with. You typically must get to a specified minimum dollar amount in the account before you are able to discuss investment options with the holding bank.

Situations Where MSA Plans Excel

These MSA plans may be appealing to some Medicare beneficiaries more than others. Here are a few situations I've seen that make these plans more attractive:

1. **You have a large amount of money in an HSA plan.** Those that go on Medicare and still have a substantial amount in a Health Savings Account often really like MSAs. First, MSA plans are familiar to them because of how similar they are to HSAs. Second, they can use their HSA money to pay for healthcare services while they let the money in their MSA account grow. When you hit Medicare, you are no longer able to contribute funds to an HSA account, but you can use the funds already in the HSA account while your MSA account grows.

2. **Those that like the idea of a $0 premium plan but don't feel an MAPD plan is the right option for them.** For instance, if the MAPD plans are not very benefit-rich in their area. Or they travel a lot and do not want to deal with networks. Neither of these issues would be a problem with an MSA plan.

3. **Those that use a direct primary care doctor or a concierge doctor.** These doctors charge a monthly premium that the

patient pays but then do not charge the patient when they come in for an appointment. These physicians will not work with insurance companies, including Medicare. With an MSA plan, you can use the funds in your bank account to pay your concierge doctor's monthly fee.

4. **Medicare beneficiaries who prefer to have more control over the funds earmarked for them.** Think of it this way: the government is going to put funds toward your healthcare on an annual basis. With an MSA, you can control a portion of those funds and even save/invest the money so it can grow. If you have a healthy year and do not spend all of the funds in your account, you get to keep them, as opposed to an insurance company pocketing those extra dollars and benefiting from your health.

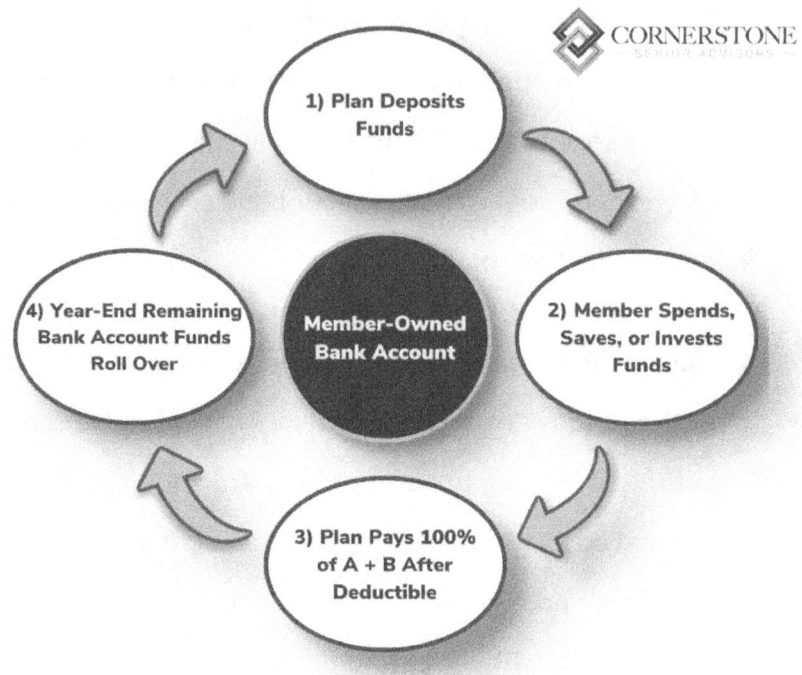

When You Can Enroll in an MSA

We will discuss five different enrollment periods shortly. However, while we are on the topic of MSA plans, I wanted to mention that you only have two opportunities to sign up for an MSA plan. You can sign up in your Initial Enrollment Period (see the section on IEP in the chapter "Enrollment Windows") which is when you first go on Medicare, or you can sign up each year during the Annual Election Period. You cannot use Special Enrollment Periods to enroll in MSA plans. An example of a SEP is if you were to move to a different state and need to change your

MA plan because you moved outside of your plan's network area. You would need to wait until the Annual Election Period to enroll in an MSA plan. You also cannot use the Open Enrollment Period (again, see the chapter on "Enrollment Windows") of January 1-March 31 to enroll in an MSA plan.

This type of plan is often a new idea for Medicare beneficiaries and can feel intimidating. I'm a little concerned putting this chapter in the book because I don't want to overwhelm you with something that seems complicated. If you do feel your head is spinning and you are a little cross-eyed at this point but are interested in an MSA, it would be beneficial for you to speak to one of our specialists. We will paint as clear of a picture for you as we can so you can make an informed decision you feel confident in.

CHAPTER 6

Beefing Up Medicare Advantage

Hospital Indemnity Plans

Indemnity means "protection or security against damage or loss." Hospital Indemnity plans do just that, protect your savings by offsetting the cost of deductibles, copays, and unexpected or additional expenses. You could say Hospital Indemnity plans are to Medicare Advantage like Medicare Supplement plans are to Original Medicare. This is just me trying to be clever, but the long and short of it is that Hospital Indemnity plans help fill the hospital out-of-pocket gap of your Medicare Advantage plans. One of the costs that often concerns people about Medicare Advantage is the amount of out-of-pocket potential if they are admitted to a hospital. If you combine an inexpensive Hospital Indemnity policy with an Advantage plan, it could potentially pay all your hospital copays for you. It works by paying you an amount you chose at enrollment for a certain number of days. We want you to be able to focus on getting healthy and not have to worry about the hundreds of dollars in bills which accumulate each day you are in the hospital.

Cancer, Heart, and Stroke Plans

Cancer, Heart, and Stroke policies are becoming more and more popular. This is a policy that will cover three of the most common health issues with very expensive consequences. The policy will pay you a benefit amount you choose when applying for coverage in the event of any one of these health conditions happening to you. That's right, this policy pays you! You can select the benefit amount; let's say you select $15,000. If you are diagnosed as having cancer or had a heart attack or a stroke, you get a check for $15,000, which you can use however you see fit.

The Numbers

These numbers are not fun to talk about, but they do help paint a picture of the value in this plan.

One out of every four deaths is caused by cancer, the second most common cause of death. 77 percent of all cancers are diagnosed in persons fifty-five or older. We all know cancer can be very expensive, not just because of your copays, but because of oral chemo medications. They can end up in the thousands a month.

Oftentimes, a lot of the costs associated with cancer are non-medically related. For example, the expenses of a specialist and of travel for treatment (hotel rooms, fuel, food) and time off work. It is easy to see how a lump sum check paid to you can be beneficial in these circumstances.

Heart attacks are the number one cause of death for both men and women in the United States. It is also responsible for one out of four deaths. Strokes are the third leading cause of death in women and fifth in men. Both conditions could lead to extensive therapy after the event, ongoing treatment, and medications that can be extremely costly. Whether you have Medicare with a Supplement or a Medicare Advantage plan, a Cancer, Heart, and Stroke policy can be very advantageous as it softens the blow of the financial impact that comes with these illnesses. The money comes to you, and you can use the funds as you see fit.

CHAPTER 7

Medicare Supplements ≠ Medicare Advantage

Confusing these two options is a mistake that happens too often. These two options are very different, with advantages and disadvantages to both when compared to each other. To reiterate what I have already said, health insurance is extremely important, and you really want to pick the coverage that makes the most sense for you and your situation. Be sure to study and understand exactly what you are signing up for and utilize the experience of one of our professionals.

Switching Between Medicare Supplement and Medicare Advantage

Advantage to Supplement

Sometimes people have the idea of starting with Medicare Advantage because it is cheaper, and they are in good health. They figure they can switch to a Medicare Supplement policy down the road when they are older and more concerned with their health. If this is your plan, you need to make sure you make the change before your health declines. When you are trying to make the jump from a Medicare Advantage plan to a Medicare Supplement, the company you chose for a Supplement will require you to answer health questions to determine your qualification for the plan. The company can deny you coverage.

Supplement to Advantage

Switching from a Medicare Supplement to Medicare Advantage is easy! The only limitation is you must wait for the Annual Election Period (October 15-December 7) in order to make that change. Medicare Advantage companies do not ask health questions or have any underwriting when you sign up with their plans.

Supplement to Supplement

When you switch from Medicare Supplement with one company to a different Supplement and/or company, you will have to answer health questions and go through underwriting. This means the company you are trying to switch to is not required to accept your application. Switching is a common occurrence with supplemental plans. Rates go up over the years and some companies tend to raise their rates faster than others. Medicare beneficiaries will often get the same supplemental plan but switch to a different company to cut their monthly premium down. This is something we help clients with weekly in our office.

Advantage to Advantage

Switching from a Medicare Advantage plan to a different Medicare Advantage plan is once again easy. You can do this during the Annual Election Period or the January 1-March 31 Open Enrollment Period. We are about to discuss these enrollment windows in much more detail.

CHAPTER 8

Enrollment Windows

Open Enrollment

Your Open Enrollment Period pertains to your enrollment window for Medicare Supplement plans when you first turn sixty-five and/or first enroll in Part B of Medicare. You can enroll in a Medicare Supplement policy up to six months in advance and six months after your Part B effective date. The great news is you don't have to answer any health questions! In your Medicare Supplement Open Enrollment window, you will automatically get approved with preferred rates with whichever company you choose to go with.

Initial Enrollment Period (IEP)

The Initial Enrollment Period is a seven-month window when you can basically sign up for all things Medicare. It begins three months prior to your sixty-fifth birthday or Medicare Part B effective date, the month of your effective date, and three months after. It overlaps your Open Enrollment Period for Supplemental plans, so you can sign up for your Medicare Supplement during your IEP. This is also when you sign up for your stand-alone prescription drug plan to go along with your Medicare Supplement or your Medicare Advantage plan.

Annual Election Period

The Annual Election Period (AEP) is basically like a "tax season" for Medicare. This is when Medicare Marketing amps up and you get to see Joe Namath, George Foreman, JJ Walker . . . even more often. AEP runs from October 15-December 7 each year. Remember when I called your drug coverage and Advantage plans moving targets? This is when we can review your plan, see what changes were made, and compare your current plan to other available plans to decide which makes the most sense for you for the upcoming year.

Changes You Can Make During AEP Include:

- Medicare Advantage to a different Medicare Advantage plan

- Medicare Advantage to a Medicare Supplement (though you will have to go through underwriting and get approved with the supplemental company you sign up with unless it is your first year on the Advantage plan).

- Medicare Supplement to Medicare Advantage
- Change prescription drug plans.

All these changes will be effective January 1 of the upcoming year.

One common misconception with AEP is people think they can only change their Medicare Supplement during this enrollment window. This is not true. You can only change to a Medicare Advantage plan during AEP. However, you can actually move from one Medicare Supplement company to another company throughout the year. Just remember, after your Initial Enrollment Period when you first go on Medicare, if you ever want to change from one company or plan to another with a Supplement, you will have to go through underwriting.

Quick reminder because I keep using the word "underwriting": This term basically means the company you are trying to sign up with will ask health questions and decide whether they want to approve your application. Don't be intimidated by underwriting. Even if you have had a health issue in the past like a stent, heart attack, or cancer, that does not mean you will not be approved. Typically, companies will just want there to be a specified amount of time that has passed since you had treatment for those events.

Medicare Advantage Open Enrollment Period (OEP)

This is not a typo; there is actually another Open Enrollment Period that primarily deals with those enrolled in a Medicare Advantage plan. This enrollment period occurs each year from January 1-March 31. During this OEP, you can make the following changes:

- Medicare Advantage back to Original Medicare
- Medicare Advantage to another Medicare Advantage plan (like for like plans)

I appreciate this enrollment period because it is our chance to "undo" decisions Medicare beneficiaries end up regretting. If you changed your Medicare Advantage plan during AEP and realize it doesn't cover your medications well or not all your healthcare providers accept the new plan, you can use this enrollment period to go to a different Medicare Advantage plan that better fits your needs.

Special Enrollment Period (SEP)

One more enrollment period I want to address quickly is the Special Enrollment Period. SEP is a time outside the enrollment periods already listed when you are allowed to make changes to your Medicare Advantage and prescription drug plan because of certain life events. Examples of life events that would qualify you for an SEP would be moving your primary residence, losing other insurance coverage, or qualifying for Medicaid. When you qualify for an SEP, you have a two-month time frame to make a change before the enrollment window closes.

CHAPTER 9

Enrolling in Parts A and B

B efore we get to how to enroll in Original Medicare, I think we should address the question of when to enroll. You are allowed to enroll in Medicare three months before your effective date. Your Medicare effective date is the first day of the month you turn sixty-five. So, if your birthday is May 15, your Medicare Parts A and B effective date will be May 1st. The only time this is not true is when your birthday is on the first day of the month; in that case, your effective date is the first day of the prior month. So, if your birthday is actually on May 1, your Medicare effective date will be April 1.

Let's go back to the example of your Medicare effective date being May 1. You can enroll in Medicare Parts A and B three months prior. So in this case, on February 1 or after you can enroll in Medicare. You have a seven-month window to enroll in Medicare. If your birthday is in May, you can enroll in Medicare anytime February through August. Three months prior, the month of, and three months after. However, waiting until after May 1 to enroll in Medicare could mean you have a lapse in health insurance coverage.

How Do You Enroll in Medicare?

If you are drawing Social Security prior to turning sixty-five, then you do not need to enroll in Medicare Part A and B because you are enrolled automatically. You will receive your red, white, and blue Medicare card in the mail roughly three months prior to your effective date.

If you are not drawing Social Security, you will need to enroll yourself in Medicare. You can do this by creating a My Social Security account and enrolling online. Another option for enrollment is to call your local Social Security office to set an in-person or phone appointment. We can walk you through your Medicare enrollment process at no cost to you and make your transition as seamless as possible by calling our office.

CHAPTER 10

What If I'm Still Working Past Sixty-Five?

Often, people are on group health insurance plans and continue to work past age sixty-five. They are not sure what they should do with Medicare. They hear they'll be penalized for not going on Medicare, but they don't want to pay for Medicare when they have group health insurance. This is a very common scenario. The most important thing I can communicate with you in this instance is make sure your group health insurance is considered creditable coverage with Medicare for both your medical and drug coverage.

You can talk with someone in your HR department or even call the customer service number on the back of your insurance card to ask this question. If your group health insurance is creditable with Medicare for both medical and drug coverage, you will not be penalized for delaying your Medicare enrollment. For most people, there is not much reason to pay Part B premiums when they have group health insurance elsewhere.

Important note: remember Medicare is unique in that your health insurance and drug coverage are viewed separately. This is why you need to make sure both are creditable with your group health insurance if you continue working past age sixty-five. Medicare will view them separately. I have worked with clients in this situation that had creditable medical insurance, but their drug coverage was not. This is not too common, but still good to check.

So, if you continue to work past age sixty-five and your medical and drug coverage are both creditable coverage, what should you do? You still sign up for Part A of Medicare. Remember, you've already paid for Part A, so when you turn sixty-five you may as well sign up for it even if you are on a group health plan that is creditable. If you are admitted to a hospital, your group plan will be primary, but Part A will kick in and help as secondary insurance.

However, you can put off signing up for Part B until you retire and actually need it. Signing up for Part B while staying on a group health plan means you'd pay an extra monthly premium for Part B when you don't need it. Why pay the Part B premium of $202.90 when you have creditable coverage elsewhere?! Also, your options when you do decide to retire can be more limited if you sign up for Part B of Medicare while on a group health insurance plan than if you would have waited to sign up for part B until you retire.

One important note: if you have group health insurance that is compatible with an HSA (Health Savings Account) and you want to continue to contribute to the HSA, you should put off signing up for Part A and B of Medicare until you retire. I will speak more about HSAs in the next chapter.

Upon deciding to retire, we tell our clients to call our office three months in advance of their retirement date. This is when we will begin getting Part B in place to coincide with when they come off their group health insurance plan.

If you are going to continue to work and your group health insurance or drug coverage are not creditable, then you will want to sign up for Medicare. There is a penalty for not signing up for Medicare when you are first eligible if you do not have creditable coverage elsewhere. This is a penalty you want to avoid because it does not go away. It will be added to the amount of premium you pay for Part B of Medicare for the rest of your life.

Weighing the Costs

It is a good idea to compare the costs of staying on the group health plan to the costs associated with Medicare so you can make an informed decision. Here are some things to consider when weighing your options:

- **Premium:** What is your employer pulling out of your paycheck each month for your group health plan, and how does it compare to Medicare?

- **Out-of-pocket exposure:** Your copays when you go to a healthcare professional, your deductibles, max out-of-pockets . . . How does this out-of-pocket exposure compare to Medicare?

- **Networks:** How many doctors accept your group health plan, and how does this compare with Medicare?

This can all be involved and maybe overwhelming. When you call our office, we can be specific to your situation and put a detailed plan in place. Then you will know exactly what to do, what to expect, and when to take action.

CHAPTER 11

Health Savings Accounts and Medicare

Today many people are on group health insurance plans through their employers. Often, the plans carry high deductibles.

These plans are considered HSA compatible, which means you are able to open a health savings account that you can use to pay for your medical expenses.

A health savings account is an account that allows you to save money solely earmarked for medical expenses.

Features of an HSA:

1. The money deposited into your HSA is a tax write-off, which means you do not pay taxes on this money.
2. Once money goes into the account, it's yours forever, until you use it.
3. It compounds interest over time.

4. You can even use it to pay for medical expenses in retirement, including Medicare Part B and D premiums, deductibles, and copays.

Many are going on Medicare with HSA accounts, which have accumulated to large sums of money over the years. This can be a blessing. However, there can be a big catch with Medicare and HSA accounts.

Working past 65 and contributing to an HSA account

You can only contribute into an HSA if you have no other health insurance besides your high deductible plan. Medicare, including Part A, is counted as other insurance. Therefore, you'd be taxed on the money put into the HSA. In short, if you have any part of Medicare with a group health plan and continue to contribute to an has, you will be penalized.

You can keep the money in the account and you can use the money in the account. You just can't contribute any longer to the account. This includes employer contributions.

This becomes an issue when someone continues to work past age 65 and they have an HSA account.

Typically, when someone continues to work past age 65 and has creditable coverage with their group plan, they sign up for Part A of Medicare because they have already paid for it. They then deny Part B until they decide to retire. Once they retire, they come off the group health plan and sign up for Part B, going fully on Medicare. However, if your group health insurance comes with an HSA, you have two options.

One, sign up for Part A, which is your hospital benefit, and stop all contributions to your HSA, including your employer contributions, so you are not penalized.

Or two, put off your enrollment into Part A until you retire. If your employer plan is creditable, you will not be penalized for putting off Medicare. This is the more popular option.

It is important to note, you cannot enroll in Social Security past age 65 without also enrolling in Part A of Medicare. Part A comes with Social Security. Separating the two is not an option. So, this creates another decision for someone on an employer plan with an HSA. Do you enroll in Social Security while still employed, or do you keep contributing to your HSA?

If you are in a position where you have already begun drawing Social Security or signed up for Part A while you are still employed, you just need to stop your contributions to your HSA. You cannot disenroll from Part A once you have enrolled.

Now, let's move down the road to when you decide to retire. It's very important to know Social Security will make your Part A effective date retroactive to six months before you applied for

Social Security. This means you must stop your HSA contributions six months before your retirement date.

How you can use an HSA account after going on Medicare

I do want to reiterate, once you are on Medicare, you can still use your HSA, You just can't contribute to it.

What can you use your HSA funds for?

- Part B premium
- Part B deductible
- Part D premium
- Prescription Drug copays
- Advantage plan monthly premium
- Advantage plan copays
- Miscellaneous Medical (dental, vision, hearing)

You cannot use your HSA funds for your Medicare supplement premium.

Feel like you're staring into a never-ending spinning wheel after reading this? It can be a lot to digest. Be sure and call our office so you can ask any questions you have on HSAs and Medicare!

CHAPTER 12

How Our Agency Makes Money

In short, you don't ever pay us a dime! When we help you get signed up with the plan and company of your choice, that company pays us for helping you get signed up with them. It does not matter whether you want Medicare Advantage or Medicare Supplement plan, they both work the same way. You also do not save premiums or get added benefits by going direct to these insurance companies. We are a resource available to you with no added expense! All these companies pay us similarly so, as I tell all our clients, we don't have a dog in the fight. We really are working for you! If one company gets out of line with their rates or benefits, we will just "fire" them and move you somewhere else that better fits your needs. We will stay in contact with you and review your coverage regularly to help ensure you continually have the coverage that makes the most sense for you and your healthcare needs.

With us, you will get claims and billing services assistance. If you have an issue, rather than calling the insurance company to try and find resolution, you can call us and we will go to bat for you!

Still Have Questions?

I tried not to get into the weeds too much in this book because I felt it could quickly become fuzzy and potentially do more harm than good. I want this book to be helpful and a blessing to all who read it, but I also understand everyone's situation is different. When you call our office, we will take a deep dive into your situation and thoroughly answer any and every question you have. We want to make your transition to Medicare as seamless as possible and be thorough in our approach.

I often tell people Medicare is the air we breathe in our office. Medicare is the world we live in each day, and honestly, we are good at it. Our goal is to be a blessing to you through the transition to Medicare or even reviewing your current Medicare coverage.

Want to get a hold of Ryan?
Email Ryan at Ryan@AdviseMedicare.NET
Call our Office at (316) 260-3331
Visit our Website at AdviseMedicare.net

You can also subscribe to
Ryan Nutter Cornerstone Senior Advisors on YouTube

Follow us on Facebook at
https://www.facebook.com/AdviseMedicare

ABOUT THE AUTHOR

Ryan Nutter is the president and CEO of Cornerstone Senior Advisors located in Wichita, Kansas. He has spent the past decade specializing in medical planning for retirement while working with clients throughout the United States. Ryan's goal was to be successful in this field and a blessing to each client he has had the opportunity to work with. Once his agency began to quickly grow, he found a lot of joy in helping other agents in the same business. Ryan now works with other agents throughout the United States providing training and council, while continuing to work with clients and their Medicare planning. He has become a highly sought-after speaker at healthcare-related events, as well as a published author for national magazines.

A Note from Ryan:

I graduated from Kansas State University in 2006 and went into ministry as a youth pastor. I then graduated from seminary and went into business! I guess I just do things a little backwards? I did not see myself landing in this world of Medicare as a kid, or really ever, until all of a sudden, there I was. Now I love it! I know if you're reading this, you're thinking, "How could anyone love a job in Medicare?" Great question! But pretty much everyone ends up on Medicare at some point, and should have someone to explain it to them. I have found a lot of joy in the service we provide to those heading into retirement and have found it to be much needed. Plus, after having twins in 2012, I don't have near the energy for those junior high lock-ins. Sixty-five-plus-year-olds are way more my pace these days.

When I talk with anyone about my business, my first response is, "For whatever reason, God has shown me a lot of favor in the business," and I would be remiss if I did not mention that here. God has blessed me and my family, and I am grateful. My hope is I can be a good steward of the opportunity He has placed before me.

www.ingramcontent.com/pod-product-compliance
Lightning Source LLC
Chambersburg PA
CBHW051537240526
45465CB00027B/606